Chefs' Special

Chicken Delight

D1410704

Chicken Delight

Chefs' Special

Compiled by
*Master Chefs
of India*

Lustre Press
Roli Books

GOURMET DELIGHT

In a land so rich in cultural heritage, it is but natural that the Indian cuisine is multifarious, offering a delight to both the eye and the palate. Its myriad flavours and cooking traditions find their roots in its historical influences. The Mughals revolutionised the art of Indian cooking with their delectable *biryanis* (an exquisite oven preparation with meat/vegetables, herbs and seasonings), *kormas* (a spicy meat or vegetarian preparation), *kebabs* and *tikkas* (meat and vegetables cooked in small pieces, usually on skewers) made in a *tandoor* (an oven made of mud and heated by a slow charcoal fire). The British Raj spawned an interesting Anglo-Indian gastronomic culture which is still eaten with relish. Different regions in India offer their own specialities with their very own taste, subtlety and aroma. The country's vast reservoir of spices made from its abundance of tropical herbs, serves as garnishing and contains medicinal and preservative properties. Indeed the range of the Indian cuisine can amaze even a connoisseur.

Chicken Delight is a multifarious offering from the four corners of the sub-continent. Be they *Starters*, *Dry Dishes* and *Curries*, you can take your pick from among a variety of cooking styles: *dum*, *tandoori* or *stir-fry*. A few basic recipes of popular cooking ingredients, including *masalas*, Indian equivalents of foods given in each list of ingredients and a Glossary of Cooking Terms are valuable add-ons. Relishing *rotis* (pp. 88-91) serve as a complimentary fillip. And to provide a finishing touch, a sprinkling of 'handy hints' are added as sure-fire remedies to common culinary problems.

BASIC INDIAN RECIPES

Green Chilli Paste
Chop the required quantity of green chillies and process until pulped.

Garam Masala (for 450 gm)
Put 200 gm cumin, 35 gm black peppercorns, 45 gm black cardamoms, 30 gm green cardamoms, 60 gm coriander seeds, 20 gm cloves, 20 gm cinnamon sticks, 15 gm bayleaves and 2 nutmegs in a processor and grind to a fine powder. Transfer to a bowl, add 20 gm mace powder and 30 gm ginger powder and mix well. Sieve and store in an airtight container.

Brown Onion Paste
Fry sliced onions over medium heat till brown. Drain excess oil and allow to cool. Process until pulped, (using very little water if required). Refrigerate in an airtight container.

Yoghurt
Boil milk and keep aside till lukewarm. Add 2 tsp yoghurt to the milk and mix well. Allow to ferment for 6-8 hours.

Red Chilli Paste
Chop red chillies and process until pulped.

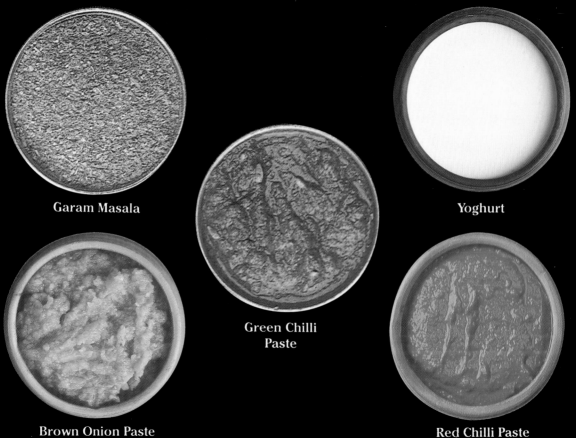

Garam Masala

Green Chilli
Paste

Yoghurt

Brown Onion Paste

Red Chilli Paste

Ginger/ Garlic Paste
Soak ginger/garlic overnight. Peel, chop and process to pulp. Refrigerate in an airtight container.

Onion Paste
Peel and quarter onions and process until pulped. Refrigerate in an airtight container.

Tomato Purée
Peel, deseed and chop the tomatoes. Transfer to a pan, add 1 lt water, 8 cloves, 8 green cardamoms, 15 gm ginger, 10 gm garlic, 5 bayleaves and 5 black peppercorns and cook on medium heat till the tomatoes are tender. Cool and process to a pulp.

Cottage Cheese (*Paneer*)
Heat 3 lt milk. Just before it boils, add 60 ml/4 tsp lemon juice or white vinegar. Strain the milk through a muslin cloth and hang for 2-3 hours to drain the whey and moisture.

Khoya
Boil milk in a wok (*kadhai*). Reduce heat and cook, stirring occasionally, till the quantity is reduced to half. Then stir constantly and scrape from all sides till a thick paste-like consistency is obtained. Allow to cool. *Khoya* is also called wholemilk fudge.

Ginger-Garlic Paste

Onion Paste

Cottage Cheese

Tomato Purée

Khoya

BARBECUED CHICKEN DRUMSTICKS

Serves: 4-5   Preparation time: 3-4 hours   Cooking time: 15-20 minutes

Ingredients

Chicken drumsticks, skinless *15*
Lemon juice *25 ml / 5 tsp*
Cumin *(jeera)* powder,
roasted *5 gm / 1 tsp*
Garam masala (p. 6) *10 gm / 2 tsp*
Garlic *(lasan)* paste (p. 8) *20 gm / 4 tsp*
Ginger *(adrak)* paste (p. 8) *20 gm /4 tsp*
Red chilli *(lal mirch)* powder
7 gm / 1½ tsp
Salt to taste
Yoghurt *(dahi)* (p. 6) *200 gm / 1 cup*
Butter/oil for basting

Method

1. Make 2 incisions on each drumstick.
2. Rub lemon juice onto the drumsticks. Keep aside for 20 minutes.
3. Add all ingredients except butter/oil into the yoghurt and mix well.
4. Add chicken to the marinade and coat the pieces evenly. Keep aside for 2-3 hours.
5. Preheat tandoor/oven/grill to 175 ºC / 350 ºF.
6. Skewer drumsticks 2 cm apart and roast/grill in tandoor/oven/grill for 10-12 minutes. Baste with melted butter/oil 2-3 times. Roast until golden brown.
7. Serve hot on a bed of shredded lettuce/cabbage garnished with onion rings, tomato slices and lemon wedges.

STUFFED TANDOORI DRUMSTICKS

Serves: 4   Preparation time:1 hour   Cooking time: 15 minutes

Ingredients

Chicken drumsticks *8*
White pepper *(safed mirch)*
5 gm / 1 tsp
Salt to taste
Ginger *(adrak)* paste (p. 8) *5 gm / 1 tsp*
Garlic *(lasan)* paste (p. 8) *5 gm / 1 tsp*
For the filling:
Cottage cheese (*paneer*)
(p. 8) *150 gm / ¾ cup*
Green chillies, finely chopped *4*
Green coriander *(hara dhaniya)*,
chopped *15 gm / 1 tbsp*
Cumin *(jeera)* powder *5 gm / 1 tsp*
Yellow chilli powder *3 gm / ½ tsp*
Cashewnuts *(kaju)*, finely
chopped *15 gm / 1 tbsp*
For the coating:
Cream *30 ml / 2 tbsp*

Cheese, grated *15 gm / 1 tbsp*
Cornflour *(makkai atta)* *15 gm / 1 tbsp*
Butter for basting

Method

1. Clean the drumsticks. Make an incision along the lower half of the drumsticks, taking care not to cut through the other side. Carefully open the flap for the filling.

2. Mix white pepper, salt, ginger and garlic pastes together and rub onto the drumsticks evenly. Keep aside for 30 minutes.

3. For the filling, mash cottage cheese in a bowl. Add green chillies, coriander, cumin, chilli powder, cashewnuts and salt. Mix well.

4. Insert the filling into the flap of the marinated

drumstick without overstuffing it. Secure the flap with a toothpick. Similarly, prepare all the drumsticks and refrigerate for 15 minutes.

5. For the coating, whisk together the cream, grated cheese and cornflour in a bowl to make a smooth paste. Coat each drumstick evenly with this paste.

6. Preheat oven / tandoor / grill to 175 °C / 350 °F. Skewer the drumsticks and roast for 8-10 minutes, basting occasionally with butter.

7. Remove skewers and hang for 3-4 minutes to let excess liquid drip off.

8. Roast again for 3-4 minutes till golden in colour. Serve hot, accompanied by salad.

❖

For a Fragrant-Smelling Refrigerator

Squeezed out lemon halves placed in the refrigerator, absorb food odours.

❖

CHUKANDRI TANGRI KEBABS

(Tandoori chicken with beetroot)

Serves: 4-5   Preparation time: 3 hours   Cooking time: 20 minutes

Ingredients

Chicken drumsticks *15*
Lemon juice *30 ml / 2 tbsp*
Beetroot *(chukandar)*, grated fine
150 gm / ¾ cup
Salt to taste
Yoghurt *(dahi)* (p. 6) *150 gm / ¾ cup*
Cream *80 gm / 5 ⅓ tbsp*
Caraway seeds *(shahi jeera)*
5 gm / 1 tsp
Garam masala (p. 6) *10 gm / 2 tsp*
Garlic *(lasan)* paste (p. 8) *25 gm / 5 tsp*
Ginger *(adrak)* paste (p. 8)
25 gm / 5 tsp
Butter *(makhan)* for basting
20 gm / 4 tsp

Method

1. Skin the chicken drumsticks and make 2 deep incisions on each.

2. Mix lemon juice, beetroot and salt and rub evenly over the chicken. Keep aside for at least 1 hour.

3. Whisk yoghurt in a bowl; add the remaining ingredients and mix well.

4. Marinate the chicken drumsticks in this mixture and keep in the refrigerator for 2-3 hours.

5. Preheat the oven to 175 °C / 350 °F. Skewer the chicken drumsticks 2 cm apart and roast for about 10-15 minutes, basting with melted butter.

6. Serve on a bed of shredded cabbage, garnished with lemon wedges and springs of parsley.

COLOURFUL CHICKEN SEEKH KEBABS

Serves: 4-5   Preparation time: 20 minutes   Cooking time: 8-10 minutes

Ingredients

Chicken, minced *800 gm / 4 cups*
Eggs, whisked *2*
Cumin *(jeera)* powder *10 gm / 2 tsp*
Yellow chilli powder *5 gm / 1 tsp*
White pepper *(safed mirch)*
powder *5 gm / 1 tsp*
Salt to taste
Oil *45 ml / 3 tbsp*
Cashewnut *(kaju)* paste
45 gm / 3 tbsp
Garlic *(lasan)* paste (p. 8) *20 gm / 4 tsp*
Ginger *(adrak)*, chopped *20 gm / 4 tsp*
Green chillies, chopped *15 gm / 1 tbsp*
Green coriander *(hara dhaniya)*,
chopped *15 gm / 3 tsp*
Onion, chopped fine *10 gm / 2 tsp*
Cottage cheese *(paneer)* (p. 8),
grated *60 gm / 4 tbsp*

Garam masala (p. 6) *5 gm / 1 tsp*
Capsicum *(Shimla mirch)*, chopped fine *10 gm / 2 tsp*
Tomato, chopped fine *10 gm / 2 tsp*
Butter for basting *60 gm / 4 tbsp*
Chaat masala *5 gm / 1 tsp*
Lemon juice *30 ml / 2 tbsp*

Method

1. Add the whisked eggs, cumin powder, yellow chilli powder, white pepper powder, salt and oil to the minced chicken and mix well. Keep aside for 15 minutes.

2. Add the cashewnut and garlic pastes, ginger, green chillies, coriander, onions, cottage cheese and garam masala to the chicken mince and mix well.

3. Divide into 8 equal portions and make into balls.

Skewer the balls of mince. With wet hands spread the balls by pressing each along the length of the skewers to make 10 cm long kebabs, 4 cm apart.

4. Mix capsicum and tomato and press over skewers evenly from top to bottom.

5. Roast until golden brown in an oven at 175 °C / 350 °F for 8-10 minutes, basting with melted butter.

6. Sprinkle chaat masala and lemon juice and serve, garnished with onion rings and lemon wedges.

— ❖ —

Pickled Chillies

Slit green chillies into halves and put them in a glass jar. Add enough malt vinegar, 1 tsp salt, 1tsp mango powder and 1 tsp mustard powder. Mix well. Cover the bottle and keep in the sun for 2 days. The pickle will be ready!

— ❖ —

HONEY CHICKEN TIKKAS

Serves: 5   Preparation time: 3 hours 45 minutes   Cooking time: 20 minutes

Ingredients

Chicken breasts *1 kg*
Lime juice *120 ml / ½ cup*
Honey *(shahad)* *100 ml / ½ cup*
Red chilli powder *15 gm / 1 tbsp*
Garlic *(lasan)* paste (p. 8) *5 gm / 1 tsp*
White pepper *(safed mirch)* powder
3 gm / ½ tsp
Nutmeg *(jaiphal)* powder
3 gm / ½ tsp
Red food colour *a pinch*
Salt to taste
Mustard oil *(sarson ka tel)*
30 ml / 2 tbsp

Method

1. Clean and debone the chicken. Cut into 2" strips.
2. Combine all the ingredients (except mustard oil) in a large bowl, coat the chicken strips evenly and leave to marinate for 3 hours.
3. Skewer the chicken strips 2 cm apart; grill / bake / roast in a charcoal grill / oven / tandoor for 8-10 minutes, basting occasionally with mustard oil. Serve hot, garnished with onion rings and tomato slices.

TANDOORI MURGH

(Tandoori chicken)

Serves: 4   Preparation time: 2 hours 30 minutes   Cooking time: 15 minutes

Ingredients

Chicken, cut into 2 big pieces
600 gm each
Red chilli powder *10 gm / 2 tsp*
Salt to taste
Lemon juice *60 ml / 4 tbsp*
Yoghurt *(dahi)* (p. 6) *150 gm / ³/₄ cup*
Oil *100 ml / ½ cup*
Ginger-garlic *(adrak-lasan)* paste
(p. 8) *30 gm / 2 tbsp*
Cumin *(jeera)* powder *10 gm / 2 tsp*
Garam masala (p. 6) *60 gm / 4 tbsp*
Butter *60 gm / 4 tbsp*

Method

1. Clean the chicken and make incisions on the skin.
2. Prepare a marinade by mixing together red chilli powder, salt and lemon juice. Rub evenly over the chickens. Keep aside for 2 hours.
3. Whisk yoghurt along with oil, ginger-garlic paste, cumin powder and garam masala and rub onto the chicken.
4. Skewer the chicken pieces. Roast in a moderately hot tandoor/oven/grill for 8-10 minutes.
5. Remove from tandoor/oven/grill, baste with butter and roast again for 3-4 minutes.
6. Remove from skewers and serve hot.

CHICKEN SPRING ROLLS

Serves: 4-5   Preparation time: 1 hour   Cooking time: 30 minutes

Ingredients

For the filling:
Chicken, boneless
(cut into 1.25 cm x 1.25 cm or ½" x
½" pieces) *500 gm / 2 ½ cups*
Oil *30 ml / 2 tbsp*
Ginger *(adrak)*, chopped
30 gm / 2 tbsp
Onions, chopped *50 gm / ¼ cup*
White pepper *(safed mirch)* powder
5 gm / 1 tsp
Garam masala (p. 6) *10 gm / 2 tsp*
Green chillies, chopped *10 gm / 2 tsp*
Green coriander *(hara dhaniya)*,
chopped *10 gm / 2 tsp*
Cottage cheese *(paneer)*, (p. 8)
grated *50 gm / ¼ cup*
Salt to taste

Lemon juice *20 ml / 1¹/₃ tbsp*
For the *roomali rotis* (6):
Flour *(maida) 250 gm /1¼ cups*
Milk *200 ml /1 cup*
Sugar *3 gm / ½ tsp*
Salt to taste
Oil *50 ml / 3 ¹/₃ tbsp*
Oil for deep frying *500 ml / 2½ cups*
Eggs, beaten *2*

Method

1. For the filling, heat the oil in a pan, add ginger and onions and sauté over medium heat for 30 seconds. **2.** Add the chicken, white pepper powder, garam masala, green chillies and green coriander and cook on low heat, stirring occasionally. When the chicken is cooked, add the cottage cheese, salt and lemon juice.

3. For the *roomali rotis,* seive the flour. Make a depression in the centre and pour the milk, sugar, salt, oil and the beaten eggs.
4. Mix gradually to make a soft dough. Cover with a moist cloth and keep aside for half an hour. Knead the dough again. Make 6 balls, dust with flour, cover and keep aside for 15 minutes.
5. Flatten each ball between the palms and roll into thin 24 cm discs or into 12" rounds.
6. Preheat the oven to 175 °C / 350 °F and bake the *rotis* on a roasting tray for 3-4 minutes. Bake on both sides.
7. Cut each *roti* into 6 pieces. Stuff each *roti* piece with the stuffing; shape like a cigar and seal edges with water. Deep fry 10 pieces at a time.
8. Serve, accompanied by a green salad.

———— ❖ ————

Fresh Milk without a Fridge

Add ½ tsp of soda bicarb while boiling milk;
it will not get spoiled even if you forget to put
it in the refrigerator.

———— ❖ ————

GRILLED CHICKEN STRIPS

Serves: 3-4   Preparation time: 6 hours   Cooking time: 20 minutes

Ingredients

Chicken breasts, deboned, skinned
and cut into strips (2" x 1") *1 kg*
For the marinade:
Vinegar *(sirka) 45 ml / 3 tbsp*
Onion (medium), finely chopped *1*
Ginger *(adrak)*, finely chopped
10 gm / 2 tsp
Garlic *(lasan)*, finely chopped
10 gm / 2 tsp
Cumin *(jeera)* powder *30 gm / 2 tbsp*
Coriander *(dhaniya)* powder
10 gm / 2 tsp
Fennel (*saunf*) seeds *15 gm / 1 tbsp*
Black cardamom *(bari elaichi)*,
ground *8*
Cinnamon *(dalchini)*, ground
5 gm / 1 tsp
Cloves *(laung)*, whole *8*

Peppercorns *(kali mirch) 20*
Cayenne pepper *(red pepper)* / red chillies,
whole, dried *3 gm / 1 tsp*
Salt to taste
Tomato pureé *15 ml / 1 tbsp*

Method

1. Blend marinade ingredients into a smooth paste.
2. Place chicken strips on a flat dish. Rub marinade on them. Cover and refrigerate for 4-5 hours.
3. Grill in tandoor for 8-10 minutes, basting twice, till lightly browned or preheat oven to 137 °C / 275 °F. Line a baking tray with aluminium foil; spread the chicken strips on the tray. Grill in two batches. Grill for 10 minutes, turn pieces over, grill for another 10 minutes until chicken is browned in spots.
4. Remove and serve on a warmed serving dish.

CREAMY CHICKEN TIKKAS

Serves: 4-6   Preparation time: 3 hours 45 minutes   Cooking time: 12 minutes

Ingredients

Chicken breasts, cubed *1 kg*
Ginger-garlic *(adrak-lasan)*
paste (p. 8) *60 gm / 4 tbsp*
Salt to taste
White pepper *(safed mirch)*
powder *5 gm / 1 tsp*
Egg, whisked *1*
Cheddar cheese, grated *60 gm / 4 tbsp*
Green chillies, deseeded and
finely chopped *8*
Green coriander *(hara dhaniya)*,
finely chopped *20 gm / 4 tsp*
Mace *(javitri)* and nutmeg *(jaiphal)*
powder *3 gm / ½ tsp*
Cornflour *(makkai atta) 10 gm / 2 tsp*
Cream *160 ml / ¾ cup*
Oil/butter for basting

Method

1. Rub ginger-garlic paste, salt and white pepper onto the chicken cubes. Keep aside for 15 minutes.
2. Add cheese, green chillies, coriander, mace-nutmeg powder, cornflour and cream to the whisked egg. Mix well and coat the chicken cubes with the prepared mixture. Marinate for at least 3 hours.
3. Skewer the chicken cubes 2 cm apart and roast in a preheated (137 °C / 275 °F) oven/grill/tandoor for 5-8 minutes. Hang skewers for 3-5 minutes to let excess liquid drip; brush with oil and roast again for 3 minutes.
4. Serve at once, garnished with chopped coriander, tomato slices and lemon wedges.

MURGH MAKHMALI KEBABS

(Creamy chicken kebabs flavoured with processed cheese)

Serves: 4   Preparation time: 2 hours 30 minutes   Cooking time: 15 minutes

Ingredients

Chicken breast fillets *800 gm / 4 cups*
Ginger-garlic *(adrak-lasan)*
paste (p. 8) *100 gm / ½ cup*
Salt to taste
Cream *200 ml / 1 cup*
Processed cheese *100 gm / ½ cup*
White pepper *(safed mirch)* powder
5 gm / 1 tsp
Green coriander *(hara dhaniya)*,
finely chopped *20 gm / 4 tsp*
Green chillies, finely chopped
20 gm / 4 tsp
Mace *(javitri)* powder *3 gm / ½ tsp*
Nutmeg *(jaiphal)* powder *3 gm / ½ tsp*
Eggs, whites *3*
Butter *60 gm / 4 tbsp*

Method

1. Clean the chicken fillets. Rub ginger-garlic paste and salt evenly on them and keep aside.
2. Mix cream along with processed cheese, white pepper powder, green coriander, green chillies, mace, nutmeg powder and egg whites. Coat the fillets evenly with this mixture. Keep aside for 2 hours.
3. Skewer the chicken fillets and roast in a moderately hot tandoor/oven/grill for 8-10 minutes. Remove, baste with butter and roast again for 3-5 minutes.
4. Remove from skewers and serve hot.

SPRING ONION CHICKEN FEAST

Serves: 4   Preparation time: 15 minutes   Cooking time: 1 hour

Ingredients

Chicken, cut into boneles
cubes *800 gm*
Mustard oil *(sarson ka tel)*
75 ml / 5 tbsp
Onions, chopped *200 gm / 1 cup*
Tomatoes, finely chopped
100 gm / ½ cup
Mustard *(rai)* seeds *10 gm / 2 tsp*
Red chilli powder to taste
Salt to taste
Cumin *(jeera)* powder *10 gm / 2 tsp*
Ginger-garlic *(adrak-lasan)*
paste (p. 8) *45 gm / 3 tbsp*
Spring onions *100 gm / ½ cup*

Method

1. Heat 2 tbsp oil in a wok *(kadhai)*. Sauté onions till transparent. Add tomatoes and cook for 10-15 minutes. Keep aside.
2. In a separate wok *(kadhai)*, heat the remaining oil. Add the mustard seeds and sauté till they crackle.
3. Stir in the onion-tomato mixture; cook for 3-4 minutes. Add the chicken, salt, cumin and red chilli powder.
4. Cook for another 20 minutes on low heat, till the chicken is done.
5. Mix in the spring onions and cook for 2 minutes.
6. Remove from heat and serve hot, accompanied by any Indian bread (pp. 88-91).

CHICKEN JALFREZI

(Chicken cooked in tomato purée)

Serves: 4   Preparation time: 2 hours 30 minutes   Cooking time: 30 minutes

Ingredients

Chicken, boneless *800 gm*
Oil for frying
Onion paste (p. 8) *100 gm / ½ cup*
Tomato purée (p. 8) *100 gm / ½ cup*
Salt to taste
Ginger *(adrak)* paste (p. 8)
50 gm / ¼ cup
Garlic *(lasan)* paste (p. 8)
50 gm / ¼ cup
Onions, diced *50 gm / ¼ cup*
Tomatoes, diced *50 gm / ¼ cup*
Capsicums *(*Shimla *mirch)*, diced
50 gm / ¼ cup
Garam masala (p. 6) *10 gm / 2 tsp*

Method

1. Cut the chicken into pieces.
2. Heat 1 tbsp oil in a wok *(kadhai)*. Add onion paste and cook for 5-7 minutes. Add tomato purée and cook for 10-15 minutes. Remove from heat and set aside.
3. Marinate the chicken pieces with salt and ginger and garlic pastes for 2 hours.
4. In a separate wok *(kadhai),* heat oil and add the onions and tomato purée. Add the marinated chicken and stir-fry till the chicken is cooked.
5. Serve hot, accompanied by a green salad and any Indian bread (pp. 88-91).

STIR-FRIED CHICKEN

Serves: 4   Preparation time: 1 hour   Cooking time: 45 minutes

Ingredients

Chicken *1 ½ kg*
Red chilli powder *3 gm / ½ tsp*
Turmeric *(haldi)* powder *5 gm / 1 tsp*
Salt to taste
Ginger *(adrak)* paste (p. 8)
45 gm / 3 tbsp
Garlic *(lasan)* paste (p. 8)
30 gm / 2 tbsp
Groundnut oil *(moongphali tel)*
80 ml / ⅓ cup
Tamarind *(imli) 25 gm / 5 tsp*
Curry leaves *(meethi
neem ke patte) 12*
Onions, chopped *75 gm / 5 tbsp*
Tomatoes, chopped *120 gm / ½ cup*
Green cardamom *(choti elaichi)*
powder *3 gm / ½ tsp*

Coriander *(dhaniya)* powder *3 gm / ½ tsp*
Clove *(laung)* powder *3 gm / ½ tsp*
Cinnamon *(dalchini)* powder *3 gm / ½ tsp*
Black peppercorns *(kali mirch)*, pounded *3 gm / ½ tsp*
Lemon juice *15 ml / 3 tbsp*
Coriander leaves *(hara dhaniya)*, chopped *20 gm / 4 tsp*

Method

1. Clean the chicken, debone and cut into 1½ " cubes.
2. Mix red chilli powder, turmeric and salt with half of the ginger and garlic pastes and rub this marinade onto the chicken pieces. Keep aside for 30 minutes.
3. Heat oil in a wok *(kadhai)*, add the marinated chicken and sauté over medium heat until evenly light brown. Remove and reserve oil.
4. Soak the tamarind in 5 tsp water for 10 minutes. Mash well, squeeze out pulp and discard.

5. Reheat reserved oil, add the curry leaves and stir. Add onions and sauté until light brown. Add the remaining ginger and garlic pastes and tomatoes. Cook till oil separates.
6. Stir in cardamom, coriander, clove and cinnamon powders along with tamarind. Cook for 5 minutes. Add chicken pieces and 1 cup water, bring to a boil and cook till the gravy coats the chicken pieces.
7. Sprinkle black peppercorns and lemon juice. Top with coriander leaves. Serve hot.

───── ❖ ─────

For Tangy Turmeric

Put small pieces of asafoetida in the container of turmeric powder to protect it from worms.

───── ❖ ─────

MINCED CHICKEN WITH PEAS

Serve: 4   Preparation time: 25 minutes   Cooking time: 15 minutes

Ingredients

Chicken, minced *600 gm / 2 ½ cups*
Green peas *(mattar) 250 gm / 1½ cups*
Butter *45 gm / 3 tbsp*
Cumin *(jeera)* seeds *4 gm / 1 tsp*
Onions, chopped *200 gm / 1 cup*
Garlic *lasan)* (peeled, crushed)
40 gm / 2 ½ tbsp
Ginger *(adrak)* paste (p. 8)
30 gm / 2 tbsp
Dry red chillies, crushed *10 gm / 2 tsp*
Salt to taste
Tomato paste *45 gm / 3 tbsp*
Green coriander *(hara dhaniya)*,
chopped *15 gm / 1 tbsp*
Eggs, boiled *2*

Method

1. Heat butter in a thick-bottomed wok *(kadhai)*. Splutter cumin seeds; add onions and stir-fry till brown.
2. Add the chicken mince, crushed garlic, ginger paste, crushed dry red chillies salt and tomato paste.
3. Stir-fry till the butter appears on top.
4. Add the green peas and stir-fry till dry and golden brown in colour.
5. Remove and serve, garnished with chopped green coriander and diced eggs.

EGG AND CHEESE-COATED CHICKEN LEGS

Serves: 4-5   Preparation time: 1 hour 30 minutes   Cooking time: 15 minutes

Ingredients

Chicken legs, skinned, deboned *5*
Nutmeg *(jaiphal)* powder *3 gm / ½ tsp*
Black pepper *(kali mirch)*, crushed
5 gm / 1 tsp
Garam masala (p. 6) *5 gm / 1 tsp*
Green chilli paste (p. 6) *5 gm / 1 tsp*
Cornflour *(makkai atta) 20 gm / 4 tsp*
Cottage cheese *(paneer)* (p. 8),
grated *60 gm / 4 tbsp*
Cream *45 ml / 3 tbsp*
Eggs *2*
Lemon juice *3 ml / ½ tsp*
Mace *(javitri)* powder *3 gm / ½ tsp*
Salt to taste
Yoghurt *(dahi)*, (p. 6) *75 gm / 5 tbsp*
Butter *45 gm / 3 tbsp*
Clarified butter *(ghee) 100 gm / ½ cup*

Method

1. With a steak hammer, flatten the deboned chicken legs and arrange on a platter.
2. Make a paste of nutmeg powder, black pepper, garam masala and green chilli paste. Rub the paste on the chicken pieces. Keep aside for an hour.
3. In a bowl combine all the other ingredients to a fine creamy consistency.
4. Marinate the chicken in this mixture for another half an hour.
5. Heat the clarified butter in a pan over medium heat and shallow fry the chicken pieces till crisp and golden.
6. Serve, garnished with lemon wedges and accompanied by green salad.

CHICKEN WITH BLACK PEPPER

Serves: 4   Preparation time: 2 hours   Cooking time: 40 minutes

Ingredients

Chicken drumsticks *800 gm*
Ginger *(adrak)* paste (p. 8)
10 gm / 2 tsp
Garlic *(lasan)* paste (p. 8) *10 gm / 2 tsp*
Turmeric *(haldi)* powder *3 gm / ½ tsp*
Red chilli paste (p. 6) *10 gm / 2 tsp*
Salt to taste
Oil for frying
Black peppercorns *(kali mirch)*,
crushed *10 gm / 2 tsp*
Lemon juice *45 ml / 3 tbsp*
Green coriander *(hara dhaniya)*,
chopped *20 gm / 4 tsp*
Garam masala (p. 6) *3 gm / ½ tsp*

Method

1. Mix together the ginger and garlic pastes, turmeric, red chilli paste and salt.
2. Marinate the chicken drumsticks in this mixture and keep aside for 2 hours.
3. Heat oil in a pan and fry chicken till golden brown in colour. Remove and keep aside.
4. In a wok *(kadhai)*, add chicken along with marinade and all other ingredients. Stir-fry till chicken is fully cooked. Serve hot, accompanied by any Indian bread (pp. 88-91).

CHICKEN CASSEROLE

Serves: 4-5 Preparation time: 40 minutes + 2 hours 30 minutes for tandoori chicken
Cooking time: 20 minutes

Ingredients

For the pastry dough:
Flour *(maida) 150 gm / ¾ cup*
Salt to taste
Sugar *10 gm / 2 tsp*
Milk *100 ml / ½ cup*
Vetivier *(kewda) 2 drops*
Butter *50 gm / ¼ cup*
Cream *120 ml / ½ cup*
Eggs, yolks *2*

Method

1. Follow the recipe for tandoori chicken (p. 20) till the chicken is half cooked—about 5 minutes.
2. Sieve the flour with the salt into a mixing bowl.
3. Dissolve the sugar in warm milk, add the vetivier and stir.
4. Pour the milk mixture into the flour, knead into a dough and keep aside for 15 minutes.
5. Add melted butter to the dough, knead again and keep aside for 10 minutes.
6. Divide dough into 2 equal portions, make a ball and dust with flour. Leave aside for another 5 minutes.
7. Grease 2 casserole dishes, one for each chicken.
8. Roll out the dough into discs, the size of each casserole dish. Prick the surface with a fork.

9. Preheat the oven to 150 °C / 300 °F.

10. Cut the chicken into four pieces and arrange in the casserole. Sprinkle half the cream on the chicken and cover with the dough *(parda)*. Brush with beaten egg yolks.

11. Repeat this process with the second chicken and dough.

12. Bake for 10-15 minutes, until the pastry is golden brown.

13. Cut open the pastry and serve the chicken along with a portion of the pastry.

— ❖ —

Lend a Sparkle to Your Microwave

To clean the inside of your microwave oven without scratching the surface, sprinkle baking soda on a damp cloth and gently wipe off the food stains.

— ❖ —

CHICKEN MINCE ROLLS

Serves: 8   Preparation time: 15 minutes   Cooking time: 30 minutes

Ingredients

Cabbage *(band gobi)*, large *1*
For the filling:
Chicken, minced *550 gm / 2³/₄ cups*
Ginger *(adrak)*, chopped *10 gm / 2 tsp*
Garlic *(lasan)*, chopped *10 gm / 2 tsp*
Onions, chopped *20 gm / 4 tsp*
Green chillies, chopped *5 gm / 1 tsp*
Black cardamom *(bari elaichi)*
powder *2 gm / ¼ tsp*
Clove *(laung)* powder *2 gm / ¼ tsp*
Red chilli paste (p. 6) *5 gm / 1 tsp*
Almond *(badam)* paste *15 gm / 3 tsp*
Salt to taste
For the curry:
Butter *40 gm / 2 ²/₃ tbsp*
Onion paste (p. 8) *50 gm / ¼ cup*
Cumin *(jeera)* powder *3 gm / 1 tsp*
Turmeric *(haldi)* powder *a pinch*

Coriander *(dhaniya)* powder *5 gm / 1 tsp*
Yellow chilli powder *8 gm / 1½ tsp*
Garam masala (p. 6) *3 gm / 1 tsp*
Saffron *(kesar)* *a pinch*
Coconut *(nariyal)* milk *200 ml / 1 cup*
Cream *150 gm / ³/₄ cup*

Method

1. Cut the stem and blanch the cabbage.
2. Mix all the ingredients for the filling.
3. Place the filling on 2 cabbage leaves and make a roll. Make eight such rolls.
4. Heat butter in a pot *(handi)*. Sauté onion paste. Add spices and cook till the oil separates.
5. Place the cabbage rolls carefully in the pot *(handi)* and pour the coconut milk and cream over them. Seal the lid and cook in a moderately hot oven for 20 minutes.

SPICY BARBECUED CHICKEN

Serves: 4-5   Preparation time: 4-5 hours   Cooking time: 15 minutes

Ingredients

Chicken broiler (600 gm each) *2*
Red chilli powder *2 gm / ½ tsp*
Lemon juice *40 ml / 2 ²/₃ tbsp*
Pomegranate *(anar)* juice
40 ml / 2 ²/₃ tbsp
Yoghurt *(dahi)*, hung (p. 6)
300 gm / 1 ½ cups
Ginger *(adrak)* paste (p. 8)
40 gm / 2 ²/₃ tbsp
Garlic *(lasan)* paste (p. 8)
40 gm / 2 ²/₃ tbsp
Caraway seeds *(shahi jeera)*
3 gm / ²/₃ tsp
Double cream *80 gm / ²/₃ tbsp*
Salt to taste
Saffron *(kesar) 1 gm / a pinch*

Black pepper *(kali mirch)*, crushed
6 gm / 1 ¹/₃ tsp
Garam masala (p. 6) *10 gm / 2 tsp*
Butter *(makhan)* for basting *40 gm / 2 ²/₃ tbsp*

Method

1. Skin the chicken and make deep incisions—3 on each side of the breast, 3 on each side of the thigh and 2 on each drumstick.
2. Mix the red chilli powder, lemon juice and pomegranate juice and rub over the chicken evenly.
3. Marinate for 2 hours in the refrigerator.
4. Whisk the yoghurt in a bowl. Add the ginger and garlic pastes, caraway seeds, cream, salt, saffron, black pepper and garam masala. Mix well.
5. Marinate the chicken in this mixture and refrigerate for at least 2-3 hours.

6. Heat oven / tandoor to 174° C / 345° F. Skewer the chicken from the tail to the head, leaving a gap of at least 4 cm between the two birds. Bake in the oven/ tandoor for 10 minutes.

7. Remove from the oven / tandoor; hang the skewers to allow the excess moisture to drip off.

8. Baste with butter and then roast again for 4-5 minutes.

9. Sprinkle with lemon juice and serve with any Indian bread of choice (pp. 88-91).

❖

If you store tea leaves for over a month, heat them in an oven at 180° C / 356° F for 10 minutes before filling them into an airtight container. This will keep the leaves fresh.

❖

STUFFED CHICKEN STEAKS

Serves: 4-5   Preparation time: 40 minutes   Cooking time: 40 minutes

Ingredients

Chicken necks, outer skin only without
the centre neck bone, cleaned
thoroughly *5 pieces* or Chicken
breasts, skinned and flattened with
a steak hammer *5 pieces*

For the filling:

Chicken, minced *900 gm / 4½ cups*
Aniseed *(saunf)* powder *3 gm / ½ tsp*
Cheese, grated *25 gm / 5 tsp*
Black pepper *(kali mirch)* powder
5 gm / 1 tsp
Butter to baste *100 gm / ½ cup*
Cream *20 ml / 4 tsp*
Egg *1*
Garam masala (p. 6) *10 gm / 2 tsp*
Ginger-garlic *(adrak-lasan)* paste
(p. 8) *60 gm /4 tbsp*
Green chilli paste (p. 6) *8 gm / 1½ tsp*

Green coriander *(hara dhaniya)*, chopped *10 gm / 2 tsp*
Lemon juice *15 ml / 1 tbsp*
Nutmeg *(jaiphal)*, grated *½*
Onions, grated *45 gm / 3 tbsp*
Salt to taste

Method

1. Mix all the ingredients (except for the chicken
necks or chicken breasts) with the chicken mince and
refrigerate for 30 minutes.

2. Divide the mixture into 5 portions and make into
balls for stuffing the breast or neck.

3. Stuff each neck right through with a portion of the
mixture and tie a thread on both ends of the stuffed
necks. If using breasts, place each ball in the centre
of the chicken breast, wrap, shape like a haggis
(heart, lungs or liver of sheep) and tie with thread.

4. Heat the oven to 150 °C / 300 °F.

5. Grease the roasting tray; arrange the stuffed necks or stuffed chicken breasts on it and dot with a little butter. Roast for 30-40 minutes, turning constantly and basting with melted butter, until the skins are golden in colour.

6. Remove the threads, arrange the chicken on a serving platter and serve hot with a green salad.

— ❖ —

Luscious Limes

Leftover pieces of lime can be kept fresh by placing them in a salt jar.

— ❖ —

SWEET-SOUR CHICKEN

Serves: 4   Preparation time: 15 minutes   Cooking time: 15 minutes

Ingredients

Chicken, boneless *800 gm*
Tomato purée (p. 8) *60 gm / ¼ cup*
Red chilli powder *3 gm / 1 tsp*
Coriander *(dhaniya)* powder
5 gm / 1 tsp
Cumin *(jeera)* powder *5 gm / 1 tsp*
Sweet mango *(meethi aam)* chutney
30 gm / 2 tbsp
Yoghurt *(dahi)* (p. 6) *50 gm / ½ cup*
Garlic *(lasan)*, crushed *15 gm / 1 tbsp*
Salt to taste
Butter *(makhan) 40 gm / 3 tbsp*
Ginger *(adrak)*, julienned (long, thin
strips) *20 gm / 4 tsp*
Green chillies *5*
Cream *60 gm / 4 tbsp*

Method

1. Cut the chicken into 1" cubes.
2. Blend tomato purée, chilli powder, coriander and cumin powder, mango chutney, yoghurt, garlic and salt in a blender to make a paste.
3. Heat butter in a thick-bottomed wok *(kadhai)*. Add the tomato paste; bring to a boil and simmer for 2 minutes.
4. Add the chicken pieces and stir-fry till the chicken is cooked.
5. Garnish with green chillies, ginger and cream. Serve with *pulao* or any Indian bread of choice (pp. 88-91).

DUM KA MURGH ZAFRANI

(Chicken oven-cooked slowly in yoghurt)

Serves: 4   Preparation time: 1 hour   Cooking time: 40 minutes

Ingredients

Chicken, cut into pieces *1 kg*
Clarified butter *(ghee)*
250 gm / 1¼ cups
Onions, sliced *60 gm / 4 tbsp*
Coriander *(dhaniya)* powder
20 gm / 4 tsp
Garlic *(lasan)* paste (p. 8)
30 gm / 2 tbsp
Yoghurt *(dahi)* (p. 6) *250 gm / 1¼ cups*
Salt to taste
Garam masala (p. 6) *5 gm / 1 tsp*
Warm milk *100 ml / ½ cup*
Water *200 ml / 1 cup*
Almond *(badam)* paste *75 gm / 5 tbsp*
Saffron *(kesar) 3 gm / 1 tsp*

Method

1. Heat 1¼ cup clarified butter in a pan and sauté onions till brown. Remove, drain excess clarified butter and blend to make a paste.

2. Heat the remaining clarified butter, add all the ingredients except onion paste, almond paste and saffron. Stir-fry for a few minutes.

3. Add the chicken pieces and cook on low heat till half-done.

4. Stir in the onion paste, almond paste and saffron, reduce heat to low and cook till the chicken pieces are tender.

5. Remove from fire and serve hot.

FRIED CHICKEN CURRY

Serves: 4   Preparation time: 1 hour   Cooking time: 45 minutes

Ingredients

Chicken *1 kg*
Red chilli powder *2 ½ gm / ½ tsp*
Turmeric *(haldi)* powder *5 gm / 1 tsp*
Salt to taste
Ginger *(adrak)* paste (p. 8)
45 gm / 3 tbsp
Garlic *(lasan)* paste (p. 8) *30 gm / 6 tsp*
Groundnut oil *(moongphali tel)*
80 ml / ⅓ cup
Tamarind *(imli)* *25 gm / 5 tsp*
Curry leaves *(methi neem ke patte)* 12
Onions, chopped *85 gm / ⅓ cup*
Tomatoes, chopped *120 gm / ½ cup*
Green cardamom *(choti elaichi)*
powder *2 ½ gm / ½ tsp*
Coriander *(dhaniya)* powder
2 ½ gm / ½ tsp
Clove *(laung)* powder *1 ¼ gm / ¼ tsp*
Cinnamon *(dalchini)* powder
1 ¼ gm / ¼ tsp
Black pepper *(kali mirch)*, pounded
2 ½ gm / ½ tsp
Lemon juice *15 ml / 3 tsp*
Coriander *(dhaniya)* leaves, chopped
20 gm / 4 tsp

Method

1. Clean the chicken, debone and cut into 1½" cubes.
2. Mix red chilli powder, turmeric and salt with half the ginger and garlic pastes. Rub this marinade on the chicken pieces and keep aside for 30 minutes.
3. Heat oil in a wok *(kadhai)*, add the marinated chicken and sauté over medium heat until evenly light brown.

4. Remove the chicken and reserve the oil.

5. Soak the tamarind in 25 ml / 5 tsp water for 10 minutes. Mash well, squeeze out the extract and discard pulp.

6. Reheat the reserved oil, add the curry leaves and stir over low heat for 30 seconds. Add onions and sauté until light brown. Add the remaining ginger and garlic pastes, stir for a minute; add tomatoes and stir. Cook till the fat appears on the sides of the pan. Add the cardamom, coriander, clove and cinnamon powders and stir for a minute. Stir in the tamarind and cook for 5 minutes.

7. Add the chicken pieces and simmer for 8-10 minutes. Add 1 cup water and bring to a boil. Reduce to medium heat and cook, stirring constantly, until the moisture has evaporated and the sauce coats the chicken pieces.

8. Sprinkle with pepper and lemon juice. Remove to a flat dish, garnish with green coriander and serve with any Indian bread of choice (pp. 88-91)

─────── ❖ ───────

Summer Cooler

Cut a lemon into a few pieces. Add 2 tbsp sugar. Fill liquidiser with a glass of cold water, the lemon pieces and sugar. Switch on for 2 minutes. Strain mixture over ice cubes and serve.

─────── ❖ ───────

CHICKEN CURRY

Serves: 4   Preparation time: 20 minutes   Cooking time: 30 minutes

Ingredients

Chicken thighs, boneless *800 gm*
Saffron *a few strands*
Refined oil *75 ml / 5 tbsp*
Garlic *(lasan)*, chopped *30 gm / 2 tbsp*
Onions, sliced *90 gm / 6 tbsp*
Cinnamon *(dalchini) 1" stick*
Cloves *(laung) 10*
Green cardamoms *(choti elaichi) 4*
Ginger-garlic *(adrak-lasan)* paste
(p. 8) *40 gm / 8 tsp*
Salt to taste
Yellow chilli powder *3 gm / 1 tsp*
Chicken stock *½ lt / 2½ cups*

Method

1. Cut chicken into bite-sized pieces. Soak saffron in a little water for 10 minutes. Crush and keep aside.

2. Heat oil in a saucepan and add chopped garlic. Sauté till brown. Add the onions and sauté till light brown. Add cinnamon, cloves and cardamoms and sauté till the onions turn golden brown.

3. Add the ginger-garlic paste, chicken, salt and yellow chilli powder. Stir for 3-4 minutes. Add chicken stock and bring to a boil. Cover and simmer till the chicken is tender.

4. Remove from fire. Take out chicken pieces. Strain the gravy into another pot using a soup strainer.

5. Cook the gravy till it becomes sauce-like. Add the chicken pieces and cook for a minute.

6. Stir in the prepared saffron and serve hot, accompanied by any Indian bread (pp. 88-91).

KADHAI MURGH

(Spicy chicken cooked in a wok)

Serves: 4   Preparation time: 30 minutes   Cooking time: 45 minutes

Ingredients

Chicken, cut into pieces *1 kg*
Clarified butter (*ghee*) *90 gm / ½ cup*
Ginger-garlic *(adrak-lasan)* paste
(p. 8) *60 gm / 4 tbsp*
Red chillies, whole, pounded *8*
Coriander *(dhaniya)* seeds
6 gm / 1 tsp
Tomatoes, chopped *1 kg*
Green chillies, chopped *4*
Green coriander *(hara dhaniya)*,
chopped *30 gm / 2 tbsp*
Ginger *(adrak)*, julienned *25 gm / 5 tsp*
Garam masala (p. 6) *10 gm / 2 tsp*
Dry fenugreek (*kasoori methi*)
powder *5 gm / 1 tsp*
Salt to taste

Method

1. Heat clarified butter in a wok *(kadhai)*. Add ginger-garlic paste and sauté till light brown.
2. Add the red chillies and coriander seeds and stir for 30 seconds. Add tomatoes. Cook for a few minutes and add green chillies, green coriander and ginger. Mix well and reduce heat to low.
3. Add the chicken pieces and cook on low heat till the gravy thickens and the chicken pieces become tender.
4. Stir in the garam masala, dry fenugreek powder and salt. Cover and cook for 5-10 minutes.
5. Remove from heat and serve hot.

CHICKEN HANDI

(Spiced gravy chicken)

Serves: 4   Preparation: 20 minutes   Cooking: 30 minutes

Ingredients

Chicken, boneless (thighs) cut into
pieces *800 gm*
Saffron *(kesar) 1 gm / a pinch*
Oil *75 ml / 5 tbsp*
Garlic *(lasan)*, chopped *30 gm / 2 tbsp*
Onions, sliced *90 gm / ½ cup*
Cinnamon *(dalchini) 1" stick*
Cloves *(laung) 10*
Green cardamoms *(choti elaichi) 4*
Ginger-garlic *(adrak-lasan)* paste
(p. 8) 40 gm / 2¼ tbsp
Salt to taste
Yellow chilli powder *3 gm / ½ tsp*
Chicken stock *500 ml / 2½ cups*

Method

1. Soak saffron in a spoonful of water for 10 minutes. Crush and keep aside.

2. Heat oil in a saucepan. Add chopped garlic, sauté till brown. Add onions and sauté till light brown. Add cinnamon, cloves, cardamoms and sauté till the onions turn golden brown.

3. Add the ginger-garlic paste, chicken, salt and yellow chilli powder. Stir for 3-4 minutes. Add chicken stock and bring to a boil. Cover and simmer till the chicken is tender.

4. Remove from fire. Take out the chicken pieces and strain the gravy into pot through a soup strainer.

5. Cook the gravy till it becomes sauce-like. Add the chicken pieces and cook for a minute.

6. Stir in the saffron and serve hot.

CHICKEN À LA MINT

Serves: 4-5 Preparation time: 15 minutes Cooking time: 30 minutes

Ingredients

Chicken, small, boneless cubes *1 kg*
Oil *25 ml / 5 tsp*
Butter, unsalted *25 gm / 5 tsp*
Bayleaf *(tej patta) 1*
Cinnamon *(dalchini)* sticks *5*
Cloves *(laung) 6*
Green cardamoms *(choti elaichi) 10*
Onions, grated *180 gm / ¾ cup*
Ginger *(adrak)* paste (p. 8) *25 gm/5 tsp*
Garlic *(lasan)* paste (p. 8) *25 gm / 5 tsp*
Turmeric *(haldi)* powder *5 gm / 1 tsp*
Red chilli powder *10 gm / 2 tsp*
Salt to taste
Almond *(badam)* paste *100 gm / ½ cup*
Cream *120 ml / ⅔ cup*
Green chillies, slit into half *6*
Mace *(javitri)* powder, *3 gm / ½ tsp*
Vetivier *(kewda) 3 drops*
Mint *(pudina)* leaves, fresh *5 gm / 1 tsp*

Method

1. Heat the oil and butter in a pan. Add bayleaf, cinnamon, cloves and cardamoms and sauté over medium heat until they begin to crackle.

2. Add the onions and sauté for a few minutes. Add the ginger and garlic pastes, turmeric, red chilli powder, salt and almond paste and cook over medium heat for 5-10 minutes until the oil separates from the mixture.

3. Add the chicken, stir and cook over medium heat for 10-15 minutes. Add cream, green chillies, mace powder and vetivier.

4. Sprinkle with fresh mint leaves, cover and seal lid with dough. Let the chicken simmer over very low heat for 5-6 minutes or keep in a preheated slow oven at 120 °C / 240 °F for 10 minutes.

5. Serve hot with *rotis* (p. 88-91).

MURGH MUMTAZ

(Chicken cooked in tomato gravy)

Serves: 4   Preparation time: 2 hours 30 minutes   Cooking time: 45 minutes

Ingredients

Chicken, cut into boneless
pieces *1 kg*
Salt to taste
Ginger-garlic *(adrak-lasan)* paste
(p. 8) *20 gm / 4 tsp*
Lemon juice *30 ml / 2 tbsp*
For the marinade:
Yoghurt *(dahi)* (p. 6), hung
100 gm / ½ cup
Garlic *(lasan)* paste (p. 8)
10 gm / 2 tsp
Cumin *(jeera)* powder *15 gm / 1 tbsp*
Red chilli paste (p. 6) *30 gm / 2 tbsp*
Oil *75 ml / 5 tbsp*
Salt to taste

For the tomato gravy:
Tomatoes *1 kg*
Ginger-garlic *(adrak-lasan)* paste (p. 8) *30 gm / 2 tbsp*
Green chillies *10*
Red chilli powder *5 gm / 1 tsp*
Cloves *(laung)* powder *5 gm / 1 tsp*
Green cardamom *(choti elaichi)* powder *5 gm / 1 tsp*
Butter *200 gm / 1 cup*
Cream *150 gm / ¾ cup*
Dry fenugreek *(kasoori methi)* powder *10 gm / 2 tsp*
Garam masala *5 gm / 1 tsp*
Water *500 ml / 2½ cups*
Salt to taste

Method

1. Rub salt, ginger-garlic paste and lemon juice on the chicken pieces. Keep aside for 20 minutes.

2. Prepare a marinade with the given ingredients and coat the chicken pieces with it. Keep aside for 2 hours.

3. For the tomato gravy, heat a pot (*handi*) and add all the ingredients except butter, cream, dry fenugreek powder and garam masala. Cook for 30 minutes, mashing continuously.

4. Strain and return to heat. Cook till the gravy thickens; add the remaining ingredients. Cook for 5 minutes and remove from heat.

5. Skewer the chicken pieces and cook in a tandoor/oven/grill for 10 minutes and add to the gravy. Mix well and serve.

❖

Re(freshen) Stale Chappatis

To reheat stale chappatis or paranthas, wrap them in a clean cloth and pack into an airtight container that fits into the pressure cooker. Pressure cook till the second whistle blows. Remove and serve.

❖

AFGHANI CHICKEN

(Creamy chicken curry)

Serves: 4   Preparation time: 30 minutes   Cooking time: 20 minutes

Ingredients

Chicken (boneless) *800 gm*
Ginger *(adrak)* paste (p. 8)
60 gm / 4 tsp
Garlic *(lasan)* paste (p. 8) *30 gm / 2 tsp*
Onions, chopped *150 gm / ¾ cup*
Red chilli powder *5 gm / 1 tsp*
Cashewnut *(kaju)* paste *75 gm / 5 tbsp*
Sesame seeds *(til)* *10 gm / 2 tsp*
Nutmeg *(jaiphal)* powder *2 gm / ½ tsp*
Salt to taste
Yoghurt *(dahi)* (p. 6) *225 gm / 1 cup*
Oil *100 ml / ½ cup*
Green cardamoms *(choti elaichi)* 2
Bayleaf *(tej patta)* 2
Green coriander *(hara dhaniya)*
20 gm / 4 tsp

Method

1. Mix ginger paste, garlic paste, sliced onions, red chilli powder, cashewnut paste, sesame seeds, nutmeg and salt with yoghurt. Marinate the chicken in this mixture for 30 minutes.
2. Heat oil in a thick-bottomed pan. Add the whole spices and stir-fry till they change colour.
3. Add the chicken along with the marinade, bring to a boil and simmer for 5 minutes.
4. Add 400 ml water and boil for 3 minutes. Cook till the chicken is tender and the gravy thickens.
5. Remove to a serving dish, garnish with coriander and serve with rice.

TOMATO-FLAVOURED CHICKEN

Serves: 4 Preparation time: 30 minutes Cooking time: 30 minutes

Ingredients

Chicken cut into 12 pieces *1 kg*
Oil 100 ml / ½ cup
Garlic *(lasan)* paste (p. 8) *20 gm / 4 tsp*
Red chillies, pounded coarsely *6-8*
Tomatoes, blanched and chopped *1 kg*
Ginger *(adrak)*, chopped *45 gm / 3 tbsp*
Green chillies, sliced *2*
Salt to taste
Red and green bell peppers
(Shimla *mirch*) *115 gm / ½ cup*
Garam masala (p. 6) *5 gm / 1 tsp*
Green coriander *(hara dhaniya)*,
chopped *5 gm /1 tsp*

Method

1. Heat oil in a wok *(kadhai)*. Sauté garlic paste, add red chillies and fry for a while. Add chopped tomatoes and cook for 5 minutes, stirring constantly.
2. Add ginger, sliced green chillies and salt. Cook on medium heat for 3-5 minutes.
3. Add chicken pieces and cook till the gravy is thick and the chicken is tender.
4. Stir in red and green peppers and garam masala. Cover and cook for 3-4 minutes.
5. Garnish with chopped coriander and serve hot.

CHICKEN SHAHJAHANI

(Chicken in a rich, spicy gravy)

Serves: 4   Preparation time: 15 minutes   Cooking time: 45 minutes

Ingredients

Chicken, skinned, cut into
8 pieces *1 kg*
Oil *80 ml / 5 1/3 tbsp*
Bayleaves *(tej patta)* 2
Cinnamon *(dalchini)* sticks (1 cm) *3*
Green cardamoms *(choti elaichi)* 8
Caraway seeds *(shahi jeera)*
3 gm / 2/3 tsp
Cloves *(laung)* 8
Onions, chopped *200 gm / 1 cup*
Turmeric *(haldi)* powder
6 gm / 1 1/3 tsp
Yellow chilli powder *8 gm / 1 2/3 tsp*
Ginger *(adrak)* paste (p. 8)
25 gm / 5 tsp
Garlic *(lasan)* paste *25 gm / 5 tsp*

Cashewnut *(kaju)* paste *100 gm / 1/2 cup*
Yoghurt *(dahi)* (p. 6), whisked *150 gm / 3/4 cup*
Hot water *200 ml / 1 cup*
Salt to taste
Cream *40 gm / 2 2/3 tbsp*
Black cardamom *(bari elaichi)* powder *3 gm / 2/3 tsp*
Eggs (boiled, quartered) *3*
Green coriander *(hara dhaniya)*,
chopped *15 gm / 3 tsp*
Ginger *(adrak)*, julienned (long,
thin strips) *5 gm / 1 tsp*

Method

1. Heat the oil in a thick-bottomed pan over medium heat. Add the bayleaves, cinnamon sticks, green cardamoms, caraway seeds and cloves; sauté until the spices begin to crackle.

2. Add onions, turmeric powder and yellow chilli powder; sauté for 30 seconds.
3. Add ginger, garlic and cashewnut pastes and sauté for 30 seconds more.
4. Add the chicken pieces and cook for 10-15 minutes over medium heat.

5. Add whisked yoghurt with 2 cups of hot water and salt. Cover and simmer for 10-15 minutes on very low heat.
6. Add the cream and cardamom powder and stir. Serve, garnished with the eggs, green coriander and ginger juliennes.

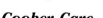

Cooker Care

If eggs are boiled in a cooker, add a piece of tamarind or lemon peel to prevent the insides of the cooker from turning black.

SAFFRON CHICKEN

Serves: 4 Preparation time: 20 minutes Cooking time: 35 minutes

Ingredients

Chicken, boneless, cut into
8 pieces *800 gm*
Oil *100 ml / ½ cup*
Bayleaves *(tej patta) 2*
Cloves *(laung) 6*
Green cardamoms *(choti elaichi) 6*
Onion paste (p. 8) *160 gm / ¾ cup*
Ginger *(adrak)* paste (p. 8)
30 gm / 2 tbsp
Garlic *(lasan)* paste (p. 8) *30 gm /2 tbsp*
Coriander *(dhaniya)* powder
6 gm / 1 tsp
Cashewnut *(kaju)* paste *75 gm / 5 tbsp*
Yoghurt *(dahi)* (p. 6), whisked
225 gm / 1 cup
Salt to taste
White pepper *(safed mirch)* powder *3
gm / 1 tsp*

Saffron *(kesar) a pinch*
Cream *150 ml / ¾ cup*

Method

1. Heat oil in a heavy-bottomed pan. Add bayleaves, cloves and cardamoms and sauté until the cardamoms change colour.
2. Add onion, ginger and garlic pastes and stir-fry till the oil separates.
3. Add coriander powder and cashewnut paste; stir-fry for 2 minutes.
4. Add boneless chicken and cook for 3 minutes.
5. Mix in the yoghurt, salt, white pepper and saffron.
6. Bring to a boil, reduce heat and simmer until the chicken becomes tender.
7. Fold in cream. Serve hot, accompanied by any Indian bread (pp. 88-91).

MURGH BADAM PASANDA

(Chicken steak with almonds)

Serves: 4   Preparation time: 1¼ hours   Cooking time: 20 minutes

Ingredients

Chicken breasts, skinned *8 pieces*
Clarified butter *(ghee) 100 gm / ½ cup*
Almonds *(badam)*, sliced
25 gm / 5 tsp
Ginger *(adrak)* paste (p. 8)
50 gm / 3 ⅓ tbsp
Yoghurt *(dahi)* (p. 6), hung
300 gm / 1½ cups
Garlic *(lasan)* paste (p. 8)
50 gm / 3 ⅓ tbsp
Salt to taste
Green cardamoms *(choti elaichi) 10*
Onions, chopped *100 gm / ½ cup*
Tomatoes *300 gm / 1½ cups*
Red chilli powder *5 gm / 1 tsp*
Flour *(maida) 10 gm / 2 tsp*

Black pepper *(kala mirch)* powder *2 gm / ½ tsp*
Cloves *(laung) 10*
Chicken stock *1 lt / 5 cups*
Mace *(javitri)* powder *2 gm / ½ tsp*
Saffron *(kesar)* (dissolved in 15 ml of milk)
1 gm / a pinch
Green coriander *(hara dhaniya) 20 gm / 4 tsp*

Method

1. Brown the almonds in 1 tbsp of clarified butter.
2. Clean and flatten the chicken breasts till about 3 cm thick.
3. Rub the ginger paste over the chicken breasts.
4. Whisk the yoghurt in a large bowl, add garlic paste and salt. Rub this mixture on the chicken and keep aside for 1 hour.

5. Heat half the clarified butter on a griddle. Place the chicken breasts on it and cook, turning over once, until half done. Remove and keep aside.

6. Add the remaining clarified butter to the pan and sauté green cardamoms and cloves till they crackle. Then add onions and cook till brown. Add tomatoes, red chilli powder, flour, black pepper, cloves and chicken stock. Cook until the gravy becomes rich and thick.

7. Place the chicken breasts in the gravy and cook, turning it over gently, for another 10 minutes.

8. Add the mace powder and the saffron dissolved in warm milk.

9. Serve, garnished with the fried almonds and green coriander.

❖

Ginger(y) clues

To keep ginger fresh, dig a shallow hole in the garden, put in the ginger pieces and cover with soil. You can use a flower pot for the same purpose.

❖

SARSON KA MURGH

(Chicken flavoured with mustard)

Serves: 4 Preparation time: 20 minutes Cooking time: 1 hour

Ingredients

Chicken, cut into 4 pieces *1 kg*
Ginger paste (p. 8) *45 gm / 3 tbsp*
Garlic paste (p. 8) *25 gm / 5 tsp*
Mustard oil *(sarson ka tel) 75 ml /5 tbsp*
Mustard *(rai)* seeds *5 gm / 1 tsp*
Fenugreek *(methi)* seeds *5 gm /1 tsp*
Red chilli paste (p. 6) *15 gm / 3 tsp*
Salt to taste
Cumin *(jeera)* powder *5 gm / 1 tsp*
Coriander *(dhaniya)* powder *5 gm/1 tsp*
Garam masala (p. 6) *5 gm / 1 tsp*
Mustard *(rai)* powder *10 gm / 2 tsp*
Mint *(pudina)* leaves, chopped
45 gm / 3 tbsp
Green coriander *(hara dhaniya)*,
chopped *100 gm / ½ cup*

Green chillies, chopped *45 gm / 3 tbsp*
Tomatoes, chopped *100 gm / ½ cup*

Method

1. Apply the chicken pieces with half the ginger and garlic pastes and salt and keep aside.
2. Heat mustard oil in a pan; add the mustard and fenugreek seeds and sauté till they crackle. Add red chilli paste, the remaining ginger and garlic pastes, salt, cumin, coriander, mustard and garam masala.
3. Prepare a paste by blending together mint, coriander and green chillies and add to the pan.
4. Add chicken pieces to the gravy and cook till the oil separates. Add a little water; cook on low heat for 15-20 minutes or till done.
5. Remove from heat and garnish with tomatoes.

CHICKEN ALMOND STEAKS

Serves: 4 Preparation time: 20 minutes Cooking time: 40 minutes

Ingredients

Chicken, escalopes *600 gm*
Egg, whisked *1*
Salt *12 gm / 2 tsp*
Red chilli powder *7 gm / 1½ tsp*
Lemon juice *10 gm / 2 tsp*
Ginger-garlic *(adrak-lasan)* paste
(p. 8) *25 gm / 5 tsp*
Oil for frying *10 ml / 2 tsp*
Almonds *(badam)*, blanched
(deskinned) *75 gm / 5 tbsp*
Yoghurt *(dahi)* (p. 6) *100 gm / ½ cup*
Butter *30 gm / 2 tbsp*
Ginger-garlic *(adrak-lasan)* paste
(p. 8) *15 gm / 1 tbsp*
White pepper *(safed mirch)* powder
3 gm / 1 tsp
Brown onion paste (p. 6) *30 gm / 2 tbsp*
Tomato purée (p. 8) *75 gm / 5 tbsp*

Cream *45 ml / 3 tbsp*
Garam masala (p. 6) *a pinch*
Cream *5 ml / 1 tsp*
Almonds *(badam)*, slivered *10 gm / 2 tsp*

Method

1. For the batter, mix together egg, 1 tsp salt, ½ tsp red chilli powder, lemon juice and 5 tsp ginger-garlic paste. Flatten out each escalope with a steak hammer and coat with the prepared batter. Refrigerate for 15 minutes.

2. Heat oil in a pan and shallow fry the chicken pieces until golden brown on both sides. Remove from heat, drain the excess oil and keep aside.

3. For the gravy, grind the blanched almonds to a fine paste and blend with yoghurt.

4. Heat oil and butter in a pan, add 1 tbsp ginger-garlic paste and sauté for a few seconds. Add yoghurt and sauté. Stir in the remaining salt, red chilli powder and white pepper powder and cook for a few seconds.

5. Stir in brown onion paste, tomato purée, 3 tbsp cream and sauté for 8-10 minutes. Add chicken pieces to the gravy. Cook on low heat till the pieces are tender and the curry is reduced to half.

6. Remove the chicken pieces from the gravy and place on a serving platter; pour the gravy on top. Sprinkle garam masala and drizzle cream. Serve hot, garnished with slivered almonds.

———— ❖ ————

Spoiling Boiling

If you start boiling eggs in cold water, they will turn tough. Place them slowly in boiling water, cover and cook.

———— ❖ ————

CHICKEN FLAVOURED WITH CASHEWNUTS

Serves: 4-5 Preparation time: 15 minutes Cooking time: 45 minutes

Ingredients

Chicken, skinned and cut into 8
pieces *1 kg*
Oil *80 ml / 5 1/3 tbsp*
Bayleaves (*tej patta*) *2*
Cinnamon (*dalchini*) sticks (1 cm) *3*
Green cardamoms (*choti elaichi*) *8*
Caraway seeds (*shah jeera*)
3 gm / 2/3 tsp
Cloves (*laung*) *8*
Onions, chopped *200 gm / 1 cup*
Turmeric (*haldi*) powder *6 gm / 1 1/3 tsp*
Yellow chilli powder *8 gm / 1 2/3 tsp*
Ginger *(adrak)* paste (p. 8) *25 gm /5 tsp*
Garlic *(lasan)* paste (p. 8) *25 gm / 5 tsp*
Cashewnut *(kaju)* paste *100 gm /1/2 cup*
Yoghurt *(dahi)* (p. 6), whisked
150 gm / 3/4 cup
Water, hot *200 ml / 1 cup*

Salt to taste
Cream *40 ml / 2 2/3 tbsp*
Black cardamom (*bari elaichi*)
powder *3 gm / 1 tsp*
Eggs, soft-boiled and quartered *3*
Green coriander *(hara dhaniya)*, chopped *15 gm / 1 tbsp*
Ginger *(adrak)*, julienned *5 gm / 1 tsp*

Method

1. Heat oil in a heavy-bottomed pan over medium heat. Add bayleaves, cinnamon sticks, green cardamoms, caraway seeds and cloves and sauté until they begin to crackle.

2. Add onions, turmeric powder and yellow chilli powder and sauté for 30 seconds.

3. Add ginger, garlic and cashewnut pastes and sauté further for 30 seconds.

4. Add chicken pieces and cook for 10-15 minutes over medium heat.

5. Pour in the whisked yoghurt with hot water and salt. Cover and simmer for 10-15 minutes on very low heat.

6. Add the cream and cardamom powder and stir-fry for 4-5 minutes. Remove from heat.

7. Serve hot, garnished with the eggs, green coriander and julienned ginger and accompanied by any Indian bread of choice (pp. 88-91).

--- ❖ ---

Oil and Boil

Eggs taken out from the refrigerator and put to boil immediately, may crack. To prevent this, add a drop of oil to the water in which the eggs are to be boiled.

--- ❖ ---

NUT(TY) CHICKEN BONANZA

Serves: 4   Preparation time: 25 minutes   Cooking time: 45 minutes

Ingredients

Chicken, whole, skinned *900 gm*
Oil *100 ml / ½ cup*
Green cardamoms *(choti elaichi) 8*
Fennel *(saunf)* seeds *10 gm / 2 tsp*
Cinnamon *(dalchini)* sticks *4*
Cloves *(laung) 10*
Onion paste (p. 8) *160 gm / ¾ cup*
Red chilli powder *10 gm / 2 tsp*
Black pepper *(kali mirch)* powder
6 gm / 1 ⅓ tsp
Salt to taste
Coriander *(dhaniya)* powder *10 gm / 2 tsp*
Poppy seed *(khus khus)* paste *15 gm / 3 tsp*
Almond *(badam)* paste *15 gm / 3 tsp*
Fresh coconut *(nariyal)* paste *150 gm / ¾ cup*
Saffron *(kesar) 1 gm / a pinch*
Cream *30 gm / 2 tbsp*

Nutmeg *(jaiphal) 3 gm / ⅔ tsp*
Vetivier *(kewda) 2 drops*
Almonds *(badam)*, fried *25 gm / 5 tsp*
Silver leaf *(varq) 1*
Gram flour *(besan) 100 gm / ½ cup*
Green coriander *(hara dhaniya)*,
chopped *8 gm / 1 ⅔ tsp*
Yoghurt *(dahi)* (p. 6) *200 gm / 1 cup*
For the stuffing:
Almonds *(badam) 100 gm / ½ cup*
Chicken, minced *800 gm / 4 cups*
Cognac (optional) *45 ml / 3 tbsp*
Cream *20 gm / 4 tsp*
Ginger *(adrak)* paste (p. 8) *5 gm / 1 tsp*
Green chilli paste (p. 6) *6 gm / 1 ⅓ tsp*
Pistachios *(pista) 25 gm / 5 tsp*
Mace *(javitri) 3 gm / ⅔ tsp*
Raisins *(kishmish) 15 gm / 3 tsp*
Salt to taste

Method

1. In a bowl, combine all the ingredients for the stuffing. Fill it into the cavity of the dressed chicken.

2. In a pan, heat the oil and fry the stuffed chicken until golden brown. Keep aside.

3. In the same pan, add cardamoms, fennel seeds, cinnamon sticks, cloves and onion paste. Sauté for 30-60 seconds. Add red chilli powder, black pepper, salt and coriander powder. Cook over low heat for 5-10 minutes.

4. Add poppy seed paste, almond paste, coconut paste and 2 cups of hot water; bring to a boil.

5. Add the chicken, cover and cook on low heat until the chicken is cooked.

6. Remove the chicken and strain the sauce; add saffron, cream, nutmeg and vetivier.

7. Place chicken on a serving dish. Pour the sauce over and garnish with almonds, silver leaf and green coriander.

---------- ❖ ----------

Mouth-Watering Milkshake

*Put 3 tbsp of any jam and a glass of milk
and blend in a mixie. Chill and serve.*

---------- ❖ ----------

BUTTER CHICKEN

Serves: 4-5   Preparation time: 20 minutes + time to roast the chicken, if tandoori chicken is not available   Cooking time: 25 minutes

Ingredients

Tandoori chicken, cut into
8 pieces each *2*
Butter *120 gm / ²/₃ cup*
Cinnamon *(dalchini)* sticks *2*
Green cardamoms *(choti elaichi)* 10
Bayleaf *(tej patta)* 1
Ginger-Garlic *(adrak-lasan)* paste
(p. 8) *90 gm /½ cup*
Tomatoes, chopped
900 gm / 4 ½ cups
Salt to taste
Water *200 ml / 1 cup*
Ginger *(adrak)*, julienned
10 gm / 2 tsp
Green chillies, slit and deseeded *5*
Paprika (red chilli powder)
5 gm /1 tsp

Cream *150 ml / ¾ cup*
Honey *(shahad) 15 ml / 1 tbsp*
Green coriander *(hara dhaniya)*,
chopped *15 gm / 1 tbsp*

Method

1. Melt half the butter in a thick-bottomed pan; sauté the cinnamon, cardamoms and bayleaf for 30 seconds. Add ginger-garlic paste and cook till water evaporates.

2. Add tomatoes and salt and cook till the tomatoes become pulpy. Add water and simmer for some time. Strain the gravy through a soup strainer into another pan.

3. Melt the remaining butter in a wok *(kadhai)*. Add ginger and green chillies and sauté for a minute. Add

the paprika—the mixture will turn a bright red. Add the gravy and bring to a boil.

3. Gently put in the chicken pieces. Simmer for about 10 minutes till the chicken softens. Gradually stir in the cream and honey.

4. Serve, garnished with chopped green coriander and accompanied by any Indian bread (pp. 88-91).

---– ❖ ––---

Honey Plus

Add a few peppercorns to your bottle of honey to keep ants at bay.

---– ❖ ––---

ORANGE RAITA

Serves: 4   Preparation time: 20 minutes

Ingredients

Yoghurt *(dahi)* (p. 6), thick
925 gm / 4 ½ cups
Salt to taste
Oranges *200 gm*
Cumin *(jeera)* seeds, roasted,
pounded *a pinch*

Method

1. Whisk the yoghurt and salt together in a serving bowl.

2. Peel and clean the oranges. Remove the seeds and separate the oranges into segments.

3. Cut into 10 mm squares; add to the yoghurt and mix well.

3. Garnish with cumin powder and chill. Serve as an accompaniment to any meal.

PUDINA PARANTHA

(Wholewheat bread flavoured with mint)

Serves: 4   Preparation time: 30 minutes   Cooking time: 10 minutes

Ingredients

Wholewheat flour (*atta*)
½ kg / 2 ½ cups
Salt *5 gm / 1 tsp*
Clarified butter (*ghee*)
120 gm / ½ cup
Water *250 ml / 1 ¼ cups*
Mint leaves (*pudina*), dried
5 gm / 1 tsp

Method

1. Mix flour, salt and half of clarified butter; add water and knead to a smooth dough. Cover and keep aside for 30 minutes.

2. Shape the dough into a ball. Flatten into a round disc with a rolling pin. Apply the remaining clarified butter and sprinkle dried mint leaves.

3. Pleat the dough into 1 collected strip. Shape into balls and roll out into 6" diameter pancakes.

4. Heat a griddle (*tawa*)/tandoor and cook till brown spots appear on both the sides.

Taftan

Khasta Roti

Pudina Parantha

Missi Roti

TAFTAN

(Rich, leavened, rice-flour bread)

Serves: 4 Preparation time: 1 hour
Cooking time: 10 minutes

Ingredients

Rice flour (*chawal ka atta*) 480 gm / 2 cups
Salt to taste / water
Sugar 3 gm / ½ tsp
Milk 240 ml / 1 cup
Clarified butter *(ghee)* 180 gm / ¾ cup
Yeast 3 gm / ½ tsp
Melon *(magaz)* seeds 10 gm / 2 tsp
Green coriander (*hara dhaniya*),
chopped 10 gm / 2 tsp

Method

1. Sieve flour and salt together.
2. Make a well in the flour. Add water, sugar, milk, clarified butter, yeast and melon seeds. Mix gradually and knead into a soft dough.
3. Divide into 4 equal balls and set aside for half an hour.
4. Dust lightly and roll into 3½" discs, ¼" thick. Sprinkle with coriander.
5. Bake in tandoor till brown.
6. Brush with clarified butter and serve hot.

MISSI ROTI

(Flavoured gram-flour bread cooked in a tandoor)

Serves: 4 Preparation time: 30 minutes
Cooking time: 10 minutes

Ingredients

Gram flour (*besan*) 300 gm / 1½ cups
Flour (*maida*) 100 gm / ½ cup
Green chillies, chopped 25 gm / 5 tsp
Ginger (*adrak*), chopped 25 gm / 5 tsp

Green coriander (*hara dhaniya*),
chopped 25 gm / 5 tsp
Pomegranate seeds (*anardana*), 20 gm / 4 tsp
Cumin (*jeera*) seeds 15 gm / 1 tbsp
Onion (*kalonji*) seeds 25 gm / 5 tsp
Salt 10 gm / 2 tsp
Butter 100 gm / ½ cup
Clarified butter (*ghee*) 30 gm / 2 tbsp

Method

1. Chop green chillies, ginger and coriander finely.

2. Crush pomegranate, cumin and onion seeds with a rolling pin.

3. Mix all ingredients except butter; knead to a soft dough with water.

4. Shape into balls and roll out into 6" diameter pancakes.

5. Cook in a griddle (*tawa*)/ tandoor until brown on both sides.

6. Remove from fire, apply butter and serve hot.

KHASTA ROTI

(Wholewheat oven-baked bread)

Serves: 4-5 Preparation time: 25 minutes
Cooking time: 10-15 minutes

Ingredients

Wholewheat flour (*atta*) 500 gm / 2½ cups
Salt to taste, Sugar 12 gm / 2½ tsp
Carom *(ajwain)* seeds 15 gm / 1 tbsp
Water 300 ml / 1½ cups

Method

1. Sieve flour; add salt, sugar and carom seeds. Knead into a hard dough with water. Cover with a moist cloth and keep aside for 15 minutes.

2. Divide the dough into 10 balls. Dust and roll into 10 cm *rotis*. Prick with a fork evenly.

3. Bake the *rotis* in an oven at 175 °C/ 350 °F for 8-10 minutes or till light brown in colour.

Glossary of Cooking Terms

Baste : Moisten meat, poultry or game during roasting by spooning over it, its juices.

Blanch : Immerse in boiling water so that peel comes off.

Blend : Mix thoroughly.

Braise : Fry lightly and then stew slowly with a little liquid in a closed container.

Croquettes : Fried mixtures of meat, fish, potatoes, etc. bound together in various shapes.

Fillet : Undercuts of loins or ribs of meat, boned sides of fish, boned breasts of poultry.

Marinade : A seasoned mixture of oil, vinegar, lemon juice, etc. in which meat, poultry and fish is left for some time to soften its fibres and add flavour to it.

Parboil : Boil for part of the normal cooking time.

Purée : Fruit, meat, fish, vegetables pounded, sieved or pulverised in an electric blender.

Sauté : Fry quickly over strong heat in fat or oil.

Whisk : To beat air rapidly into a mixture with an egg rotary or electric beater.

Fold : Mix one ingredient with another using a gentle cutting and turning motion.

Beat : Agitate a mixture by vigorously turning it over with an upward movement to introduce air; a spoon, fork, whisk or electric mixer may be used.

Stir-fry : Fry rapidly while stirring and tossing.

Stock : Liquid produced when meat, poultry, bones, vegetables are simmered in water with herbs and flavourings for several hours.

Simmer : Keep boiling gently on low heat.

INDEX

STARTERS

DRY DISHES

CURRIES

ACCOMPANIMENTS

Acknowledgements

Grateful thanks to the Master Chefs at **The Intercontinental Hotel,** New Delhi, and the **Oberoi Group of Hotels,** New Delhi, for making available their kitchens for the preparation and photography of the dishes.

ISBN: 81-7436-072-7

Third impression 2002

© Roli & Janssen BV
Published in India by Roli Books in arrangement with Roli & Janssen BV
M 75, Greater Kailash II Market, New Delhi-110 048, INDIA
Tel.: (011) 6442271, 6462782, Fax: (011) 6467185
E-mail: roli@vsnl.com, Website: rolibooks.com

Photographs: Dheeraj Paul

Printed in Singapore